GOVERNMENT FOR KIDS
CITIZENSHIP TO GOVERNANCE

STATE AND FEDERAL PUBLIC ADMINISTRATION
3RD GRADE SOCIAL STUDIES

BABY PROFESSOR
EDUCATION KIDS

Speedy Publishing LLC
40 E. Main St. #1156
Newark, DE 19711
www.speedypublishing.com
Copyright 2017

In this book, we're going to talk about what it means to be a United States citizen and how the federal government and the state governments operate. So, let's get right to it!

WHAT DOES IT MEAN TO BE A CITIZEN?

Every United States citizen is given rights, and along with those rights come responsibilities. The United States is frequently referred to as a "melting pot." This simply means that the United States has welcomed people from every nation on Earth. The citizens of the United States come from all different races, religions, countries, and walks of life.

Grand Central Terminal

New York Public Library

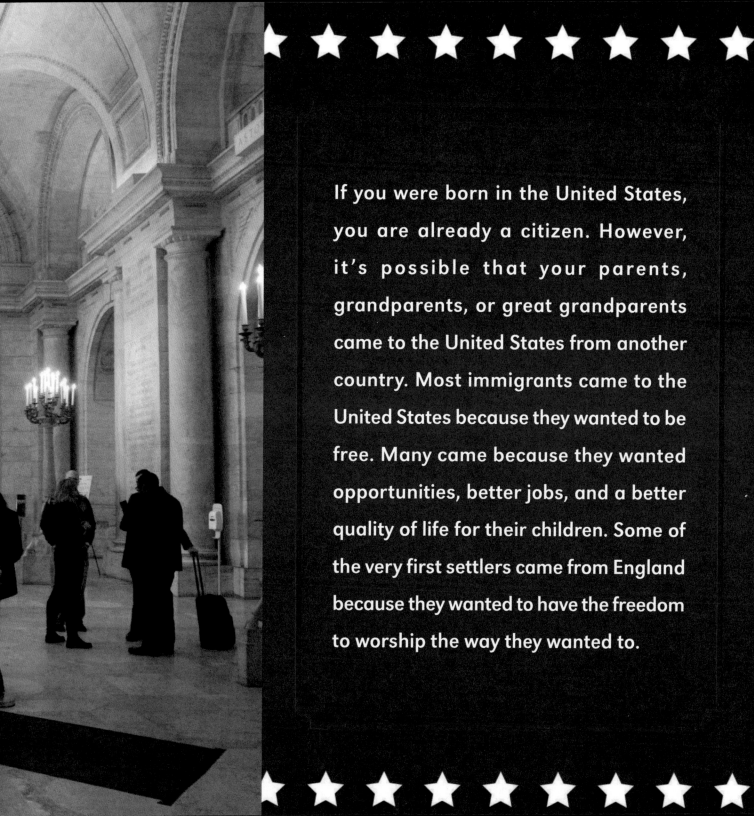

If you were born in the United States, you are already a citizen. However, it's possible that your parents, grandparents, or great grandparents came to the United States from another country. Most immigrants came to the United States because they wanted to be free. Many came because they wanted opportunities, better jobs, and a better quality of life for their children. Some of the very first settlers came from England because they wanted to have the freedom to worship the way they wanted to.

WHAT RIGHTS DOES A CITIZEN HAVE?

A citizen of the United States has more freedom than citizens in many other countries.

Here are some of these freedoms:

The right to cast votes in federal and local elections

The right to pursue your own personal and business goals that you feel will lead you to happiness

The right to a speedy, fair trial by a jury made up of people like you.

The right to worship whichever religion you see fit.

WHAT RESPONSIBILITIES DOES A CITIZEN HAVE?

A United States citizen is expected to perform duties and handle responsibilities as well.

United States Capitol

Here are some of these responsibilities:

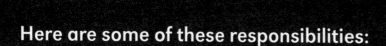 The responsibility of supporting as well as defending the information presented in the United States Constitution

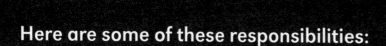 The responsibility of being an active participant in the process of democracy

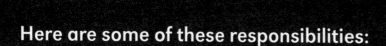 The responsibility of staying well informed on the issues of your community as well as the issues of the country

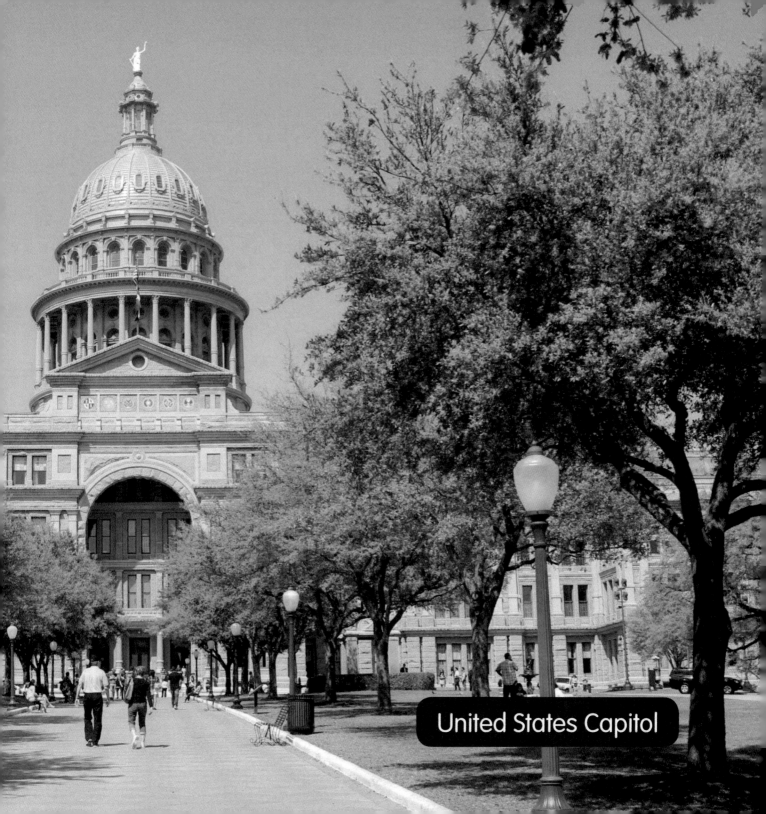

United States Capitol

- The responsibility of paying your federal taxes and state taxes on time and with honesty
- The responsibility of helping to defend the country from foreign invaders should it become necessary
- The responsibility of being part of a jury when called upon to do so
- The responsibility of respecting others and not discriminating against them for their race, religion, or opinions

IF YOU ARE FROM A FOREIGN COUNTRY CAN YOU BECOME A UNITED STATES CITIZEN?

If you were born in the United States, then you are considered a "native' citizen. There are still many people who come to the United States from foreign countries. Some people cross the border illegally and are sometimes sent back if they are caught. Others apply legally for "Green Cards" that allow them to live and work in the United States. Once a person has lived legally in the United States for five years, then, he or she can apply to go through the process of becoming a citizen, which is called naturalization. If the immigrant is married to a United States citizen, he or she can apply to become a citizen after living in the United States legally for three years.

Grand Central Terminal

A person applying for citizenship must be at least 18 years of age and have a good character. He or she must have a good command of the English language. Also, the potential citizen must be able to pledge loyalty to the United States by taking an oath.

STEPS TO CITIZENSHIP

Once individuals have fulfilled the previous requirements, there are a series of other steps they must follow to become citizens. Here are those steps:

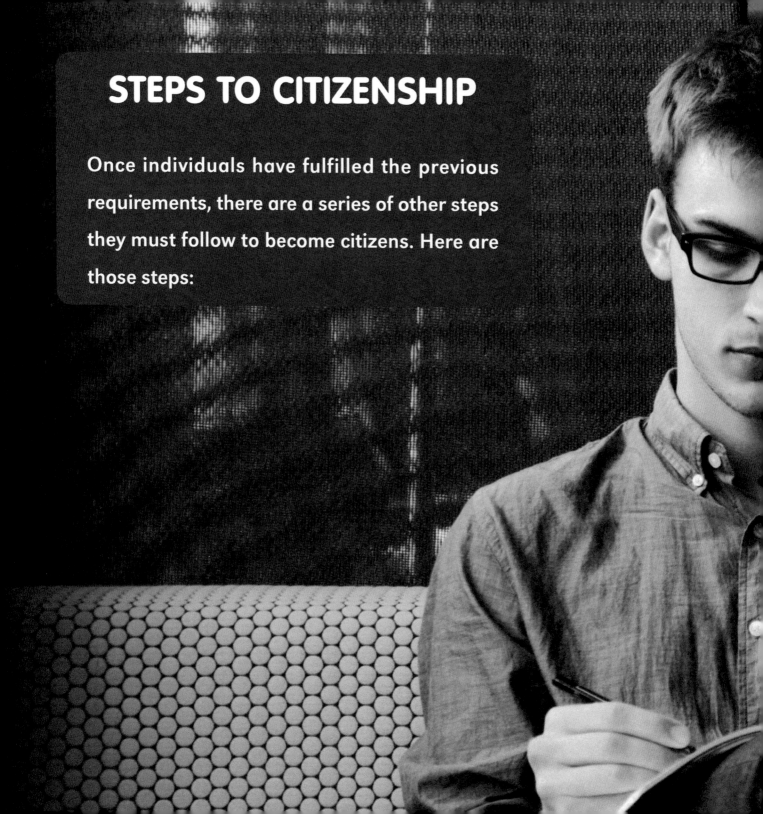

They must fill out a form called the N-400 form, which is processed by the USCIS, the United States Citizenship and Immigration Services department.

Sometimes it takes more than a year to get a reply. There are hundreds of thousands of applications to process.

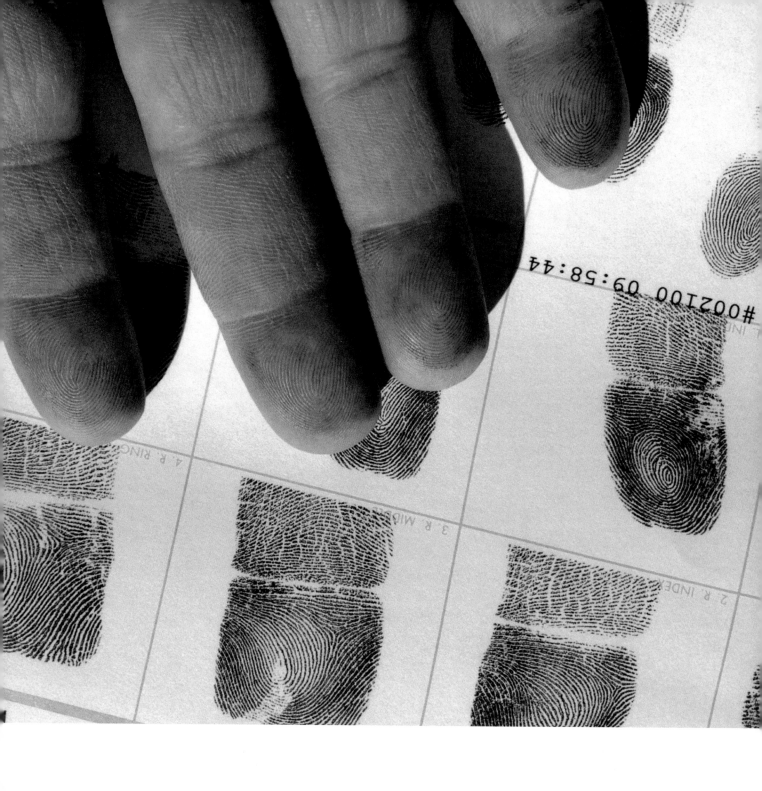

They must be fingerprinted and their fingerprints will be reviewed by the Federal Bureau of Investigation to ensure that they haven't been involved in criminal activity.

They are interviewed by an officer from the immigration department and asked many personal questions about their careers, their families, and their backgrounds. They will take a test for reading and writing English. They will also be asked questions about important historical events in the United States or questions about how the government operates. They will be given material to use as they study for this test. Some possible questions might be: What are the Articles of Confederation? What is the Bill of Rights? How many branches of the federal government are there and what are their names?

The final step is taking an oath that ensures that as a US citizen they will be loyal to the United States, obey the tenets of the US Constitution, and be willing to defend the United States. This oath is made in a courtroom in the presence of many other people. Then, they will receive a certificate that states they are naturalized and are now officially a United States citizen.

HOW DOES THE FEDERAL GOVERNMENT OPERATE?

The United States Constitution divides the government into three separate branches. There is an executive branch, which is the head of the government. The two other branches, the legislative and the judiciary, ensure that the President doesn't become too powerful. This system, where all three divisions keep the power in balance, is called the system of "checks and balances."

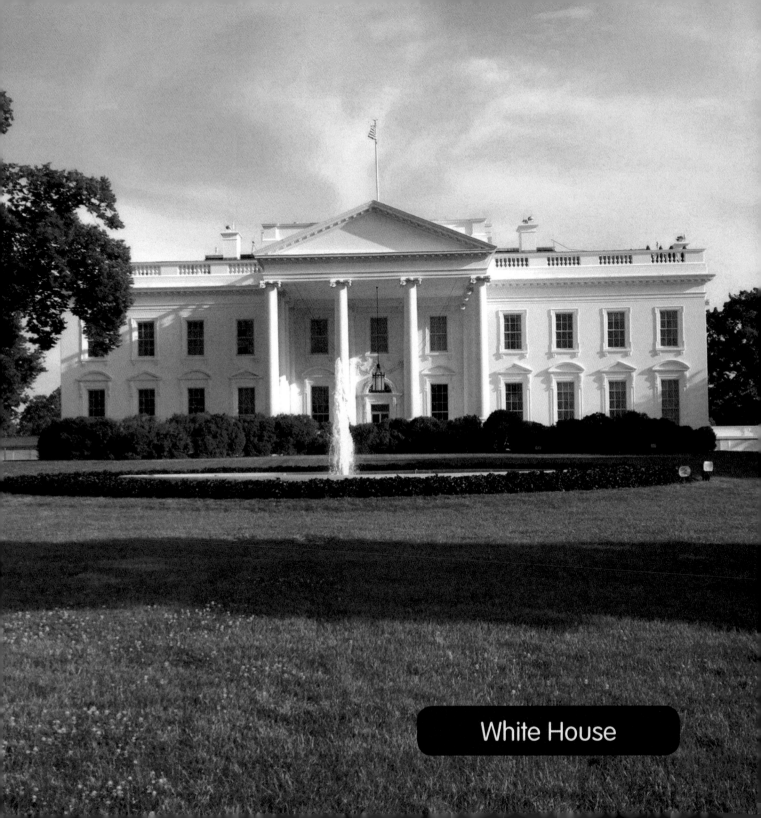

White House

White House

The Founding Fathers didn't want the President to be a monarch like the rulers in Great Britain. By establishing three branches, they could be assured that no one segment of the government would get too powerful.

THE EXECUTIVE BRANCH

This branch is composed of the President and the President's advisors including the Vice President, the Cabinet, and the EOP, which is the Executive Office of the President. The EOP includes the staff of the White House and other positions that are hired by the President or approved by the Senate. The President has lots of roles to fill. He or she leads the United States government. The President is also considered the head of state in working with other countries. Another important role of the President is to be commander of all the armed forces.

United States Capitol

United States Capitol

Some of the President's responsibilities are:

➥ To approve or veto laws proposed by Congress

➥ To enforce the laws that have been approved

➥ To work with other nations to establish trade relations and other global policies

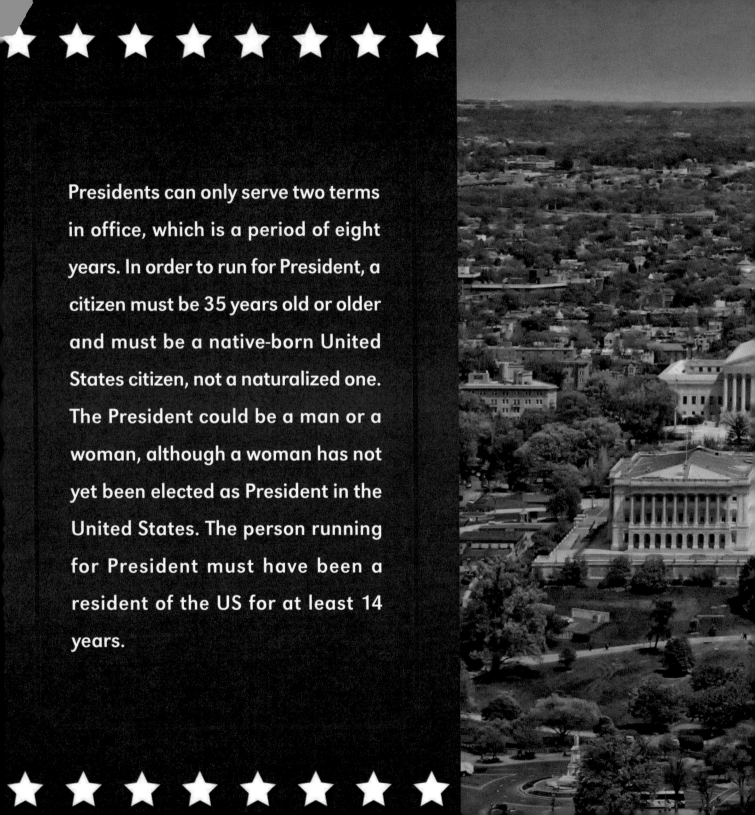

Presidents can only serve two terms in office, which is a period of eight years. In order to run for President, a citizen must be 35 years old or older and must be a native-born United States citizen, not a naturalized one. The President could be a man or a woman, although a woman has not yet been elected as President in the United States. The person running for President must have been a resident of the US for at least 14 years.

United States Capitol

US Supreme Court

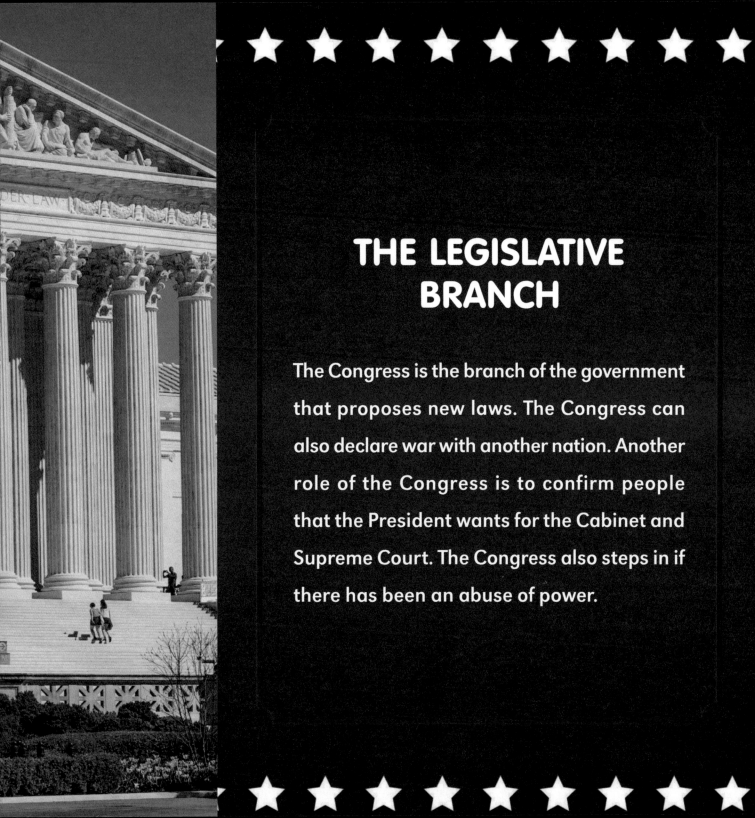

THE LEGISLATIVE BRANCH

The Congress is the branch of the government that proposes new laws. The Congress can also declare war with another nation. Another role of the Congress is to confirm people that the President wants for the Cabinet and Supreme Court. The Congress also steps in if there has been an abuse of power.

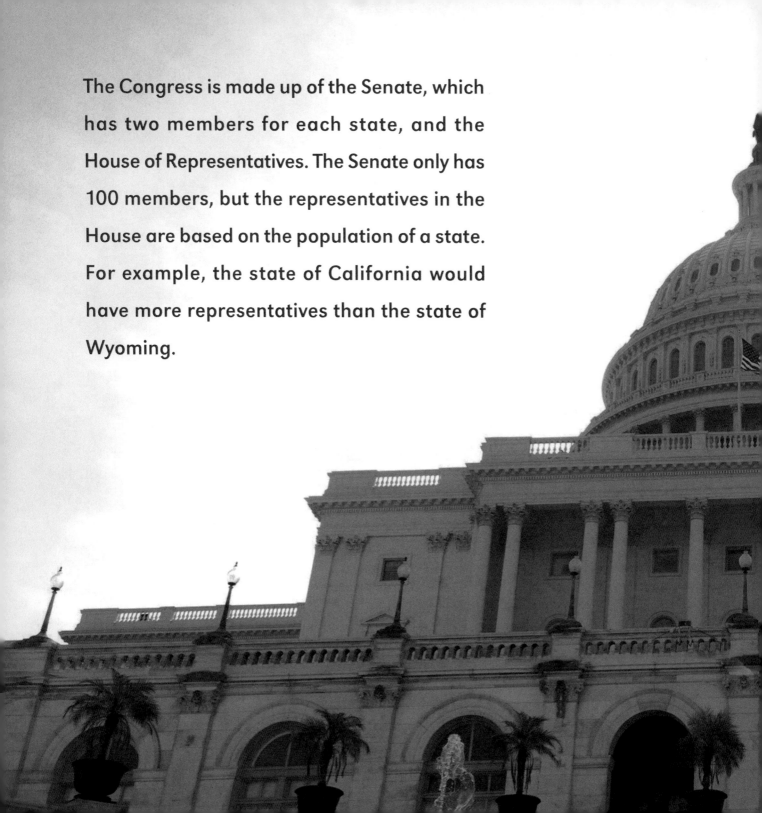

The Congress is made up of the Senate, which has two members for each state, and the House of Representatives. The Senate only has 100 members, but the representatives in the House are based on the population of a state. For example, the state of California would have more representatives than the state of Wyoming.

United States Capitol

US Supreme Court

THE JUDICIAL BRANCH

This branch of the government is the court system. They don't enact laws, but they do interpret them. The President appoints Federal judges and then the Senate decides whether to approve them. The most important court in the land is the United States Supreme Court. The members of the Supreme Court have the final say on any decision and their cases cannot be appealed.

The next set of important courts are the Courts of Appeals. There are thirteen Courts of Appeals. At the lowest level of federal courts are the ninety-four United States District Courts. Federal judges keep their jobs their entire lives unless the Congress decides to impeach them. One of the reasons for this is so they can judge based on what they feel is right, not what they have to do to become elected.

New York City Hall

United States Capitol

HOW DO STATE GOVERNMENTS OPERATE?

Each state has a constitution that explains the state's laws that are not determined by the US Constitution or the federal government. Each state has a head government official, called a governor. The governor's advisors may include a lieutenant governor as well as an attorney general and a secretary of state.

The state's legislature proposes and approves the state's laws and every state with the exception of Nebraska has two houses, just like Congress. The judicial branch at the state level also has a Supreme Court for the state with lower courts to handle everyday cases.

US Supreme Court lobby

SUMMARY

Citizens of the United States have many more freedoms than citizens in other countries. Hundreds of thousands of people from all over the world apply for United States citizenship every year. The United States government is set up on a system of checks and balances with executive, legislative, and judiciary branches. States have their own constitutions and are modeled on the same three divisions of power as the federal government.

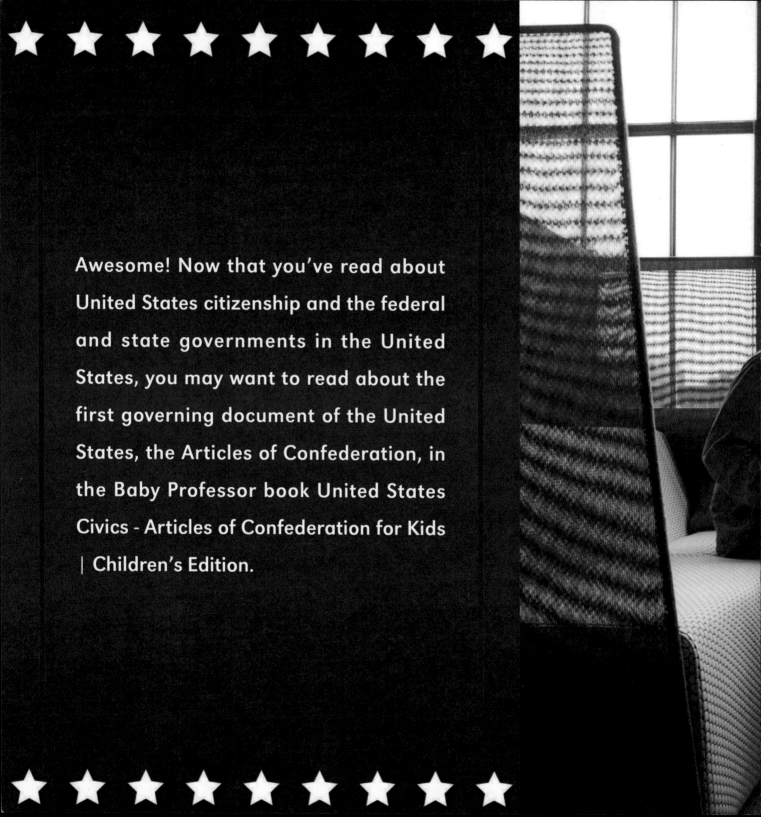

Awesome! Now that you've read about United States citizenship and the federal and state governments in the United States, you may want to read about the first governing document of the United States, the Articles of Confederation, in the Baby Professor book United States Civics - Articles of Confederation for Kids | Children's Edition.

Visit

BABY PROFESSOR
EDUCATION KIDS

www.BabyProfessorBooks.com

to download Free Baby Professor eBooks
and view our catalog of new and exciting
Children's Books

Made in the USA
Las Vegas, NV
21 September 2023

77908042R00040